The Female Semaphore

THE FEMALE SEMAPHORE

First published in New Zealand by CheekyBird Press in 2005

This edition published in 2018

Published by:
    CheekyBird Press
    PO Box 104
    Taupo, New Zealand
    E-mail: frontdesk@magari.co.nz
    www.magari.co.nz

ISBN: 978-0-908801-65-7 2018 Print edition
        9780908801664 Ebook

the

FEMALE
SEMAPHORE

communication

Margaret Woodhouse

CheekyBird Press

Contents

Contents

Now—let me tell you all about it...

Female Semaphore

Female semaphore is the ultimate means of communication. Since the men and children in your life don't listen, trying to be heard can be frustrating in the extreme. But as long as you can be seen you do not need to be heard. The technique is easily learned, quickly understood. Women will immediately recognise the signals and find them easy to repeat. Using them in the correct situations will ensure a more fulfilling relationship with those around you.

But this is not simply a good thing for women. Children and men can also benefit. By learning to interpret the signals and knowing how to respond to them their lives will improve immeasurably.

The benefits of clear signalling have been recognised through the millennia. Strong women have taken advantage of visual

messaging and reaped the rewards.

Foolish women have in turn learned bitter lessons as a consequence of having ignored some basic signalling rules.

Be strong not foolish! Equip yourself for success in life by learning female semaphore now.

Female semaphore has a number of standard signals. Learn these first. Once mastered you will discover just how adaptable female semaphore can be. Before long you will be using more and more complex signalling. It is such a fluid language you will soon be developing your own new signals to share with those around you.

After all, being fluid with signals is what being female is all about.

The Qualified Female Semaphorist

1. Attributes

A competent signaller can be any size, age or shape, but must be female. And since maturity in the signaller is also requisite, the presence of boobs immediately identifies a qualified semaphorist.

Dexterity is always a bonus but not a necessity. If you find signalling doesn't come naturally, try practising to music. Perfect is Vivaldi's *Four Seasons' Winter*. This is a movement with plenty of the same desperate energy out of which signalling is born. Recordings are infuriatingly available.

2. Visibility

Do not be reticent, modest or considerate.

In-your-face is what female semaphore is all about. There is nothing less effective than an apologetic signaller.

3. Clothing

It is always a good idea to be wearing appropriate clothing. What could be worse, when communicating calm in the face of adversity, than getting caught in the middle of flexing that critical sinew only to find that your fab D&G pants have split and one of those boobs is left hanging out of the top?

4. Timing

When applying female semaphore, patience is no virtue. Don't wait for the 'right' moment or the impact of what it is you have to communicate might be lost.

5. Read on…

for the step by step guide to female semaphore. PLUS: learn about some famous female semaphorists and the consequences of female semaphore in true-life action.

Semaphore #1

APPLICATION: Use this signal for multiple communications of the best news, such as: you've thought of a great family outing; the results of your pregnancy test are negative; the kids have just reached dish washing maturity; you've made it through menopause.

SEMAPHORE ACTION: Raise arms to represent general jubilation. Hands are open and joyous. Your enthusiasm will go unrewarded for a considerable duration, so make sure feet are kept firm and steady. (**Recipients**: Display an equal enthusiasm or you'll end up having to put up with more of the same.)

TFS TIP

Sometimes conventional, verbal communication with the men and children in your life becomes an absolute necessity. Don't hold back! Use The Female Semaphore *Let's Chat* signals liberally. Soon you will be provoking considerable comment from your loved ones and conversation will once more echo around the home. Think about it! They'll talk simply to get rid of you.

Guess what!

INTERPRETATION:
I'm making an effort so for heaven's sake react by talking to me.

Semaphore #2

APPLICATION: Use this signal for multiple communications of the worst news, such as: the basin's covered in whiskers—again; the clothes need washing—again; the football season's started—again; the twins have been expelled from day care.

SEMAPHORE ACTION: Telescope head forward and tilt lips slightly to indicate hopelessness. Allow shoulders to slump and hands to fall limp. Direct eyes meaningfully. (**Recipients** take note: Wipe that smile of pseudo understanding. She means YOUR: whiskers; clothes; football obsession; twins.)

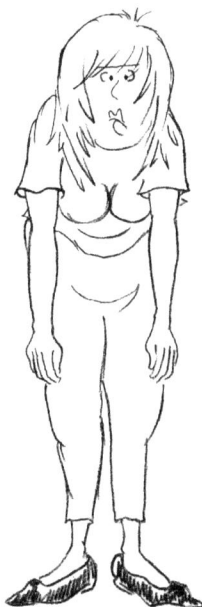

Guess what?

INTERPRETATION:
I really *do* want you to say, "You poor old thing. How can I help?"

Semaphore #3

APPLICATION: Female Semaphorists should only bother with this signal to compel the Recipient to react *constructively* to such verbal questions as: hey, didn't we agree to watch my programme tonight; hey, where have you put the keys this time; hey, what's more important, the football or the twins?

SEMAPHORE ACTION: Lift bosom with folded arms to form prominent escarpment. Neck is telescoped into serious shoulders and nostrils are flared with purpose.

How to Signal the Need to Chat 3

Hey!

INTERPRETATION:
I've asked the question and failure to render a verbal answer will result in the most appalling consequences.

Let's Chat
Combination Semaphore

PRACTICE NOTES: Hopefully you have now had a chance to practise Semaphores #1–3 and you are becoming familiar with The Female Semaphore style of communication. As you advance through each semaphore step you will become more skilled and will learn how to use the semaphores in whole sentences for extra effect.

The combination semaphore opposite is your first practice using a full sentence. Note carefully how the signals run together. "Guess what" is signalled to gain initial attention. Once he's all yours, express the second semaphore. And how could he not be sympathetic when he sees you move into such a telling final semaphore.

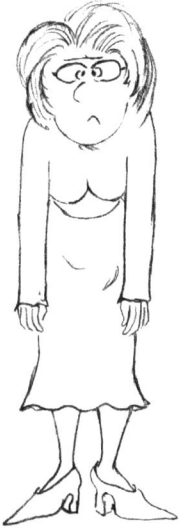

Guess what?

The kids have rung and...

...they've quit the flat and are moving back home to live!

Semaphore #4

APPLICATION: Use this signal as a defiant gesture to communicate such critical messages as: she might have big boobs but my curves are better; she's probably drunk; so what if she not only looks like that but she's got a double PhD as well; isn't that a face lift?

SEMAPHORE ACTION: With left shoulder well raised the back must be slightly turned. Feet should be used to gain additional status. Hold drink, if you have one, confidently in right hand. (And see pages 36–39.)

TES TIP

Let's face it, girls, they are wrong and you are right—it's just that they don't see it that way. Become well versed in the *let's-get-this-straight* signals. They arm you with the ultimate in female weaponry—the *last* word. Watch the Recipients buckle under the onslaught.

What makes you think...

INTERPRETATION:
You really don't know my full measure, do you? Well get this...

Semaphore #5

APPLICATION: This is an emergency signal and should be used sparingly and *never* lightly to impart such advice as: you could well have meant that, and I am magnanimous enough to consider admitting that I might have, inadvertently, mind, *possibly* said what you suggest I said... maybe.

SEMAPHORE ACTION: Both arms straight and hands held abject as in a prelude to an admission of possible wrong (though not definitely). You are on the back foot. **(RECIPIENTS:** That sanctimony you are currently displaying as you read this has no place here. You're riding for a fall.)

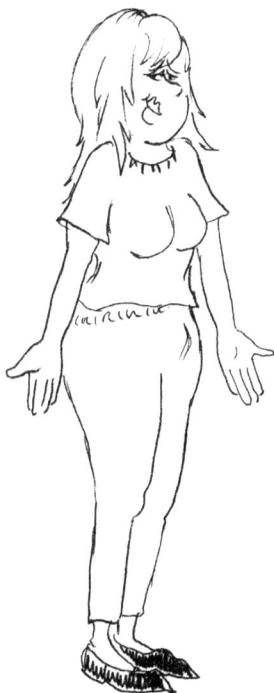

What I said was...

INTERPRETATION:
All of us are human—but only sometimes.

Semaphore #6

APPLICATION: Use this signal as a defiant gesture to communicate such critical messages as: nothing will make me change my mind; we've been through this countless times before; that may be what I *said* but it obviously wasn't what I *meant;* are you deaf or something? (Use this signal liberally once sufficient time has lapsed since you exercised Semaphore #5.)

SEMAPHORE ACTION: With head on a left-hand tilt of generous understanding, and right shoulder sliding, hands are splayed outward to indicate superiority. Wait until Recipient is watching then establish your balance firmly on your front foot.

What I *actually* said was...

INTERPRETATION:
That's maybe what you thought you heard…
but you can't have understood what you heard correctly.

Practice Makes Perfect

How are you getting on? A little exhausted trying to get your head around all this signalling? Or perhaps you are already exhilarated by these wonderful affirmations you've been waiting years to display. Think of it girls! With female semaphore you get to communicate *and* do a full work-out at the very same time.

Female semaphore is the *How to* in: How to stay physically and mentally healthy and enjoy yourself while keeping the men and children in your life under control, the laundry out of the laundry basket, the dog washed, and the cat fed. And all this without having to utter a single word.

Practise semaphores in front of the mirror *ev-er-y* day, and don't be afraid to put your new skills to work. Some time when you think you're ready, experiment with the combination semaphores on the following pages. But first try out the TFS Work Out (pages 27 through 35)—recommended by Brad Limplater, TFS Work Out Coach to the Stars.

The TFS Work Out

BRAD LIMPLATER'S
SEMAPHORE WORK OUT CHANT

Stretch—and shrug.
Stretch—and hug.
Clear the fug—and feel
Conf-i-dent and smug.

Brad says:

Work on that pout, there's nothing better than a pursed lip for getting the message across. This message is: "I'm fab".

TFS WO1:

strike pose 10x daily.

TFS Work Out 1

Brad says:

Stay puckered up, you're about
to go coy. This is your signal for:
"approach at your own risk."

TFS WO2:

strike pose 8x daily.

TFS Work Out 2

Brad says:

This is the ultimate and relies on the California Body Axis, that is: breast, lips, right knee, and pelvis forward, all else back. Start with head facing the front and turn to use facial expressions to signal your Phrase of the Day.*

TFS WO3:

strike pose endlessly daily.

* The Phrase of the Day is dictated by your menstrual cycle. The example illustrated is the *Ovulation come-hither*. A clever lowering of the eyebrows would immediately render it the *PMT brush-off*.

TFS WORK OUT 3

Brad says:

Personally he would rather have nothing to do with this un-Star like pose. However, we include it as a natural conclusion to such a strenuous work out. It's what you deserve, a rare signal to yourself to say "enough is enough".

TFS WO4:

strike pose once daily at end of work out.

TFS WORK OUT 4

SET THE RECORD STRAIGHT
COMBINATION SEMAPHORE 1

PRACTICE NOTES: Here's another sentence to try out. In this sentence you will demonstrate your true abandon.

Executing these semaphores together has two advantages. The first semaphore renders the Recipient insecure and guilty. Guilt is an indispensable weapon in the fight for control. The second semaphore then establishes your sexual prowess—a powerful tool when handling a Recipient who has been rendered insecure and guilty.

To ensure accurate interpretation of this combination semaphore, think flamenco!

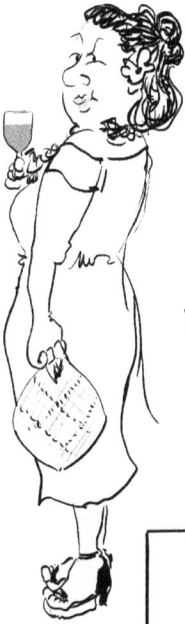

What makes you think...

...I haven't got what she's got!

SET THE RECORD STRAIGHT
COMBINATION SEMAPHORE 2

PRACTICE NOTES: Let's try another sentence with another model—this time, from true abandon to the ultimate let down. This combination semaphore is for those times when pay-back seems called for.

Observe carefully our model's posture in the second semaphore; body generally electrifies into high sexual prowess—head on the slight tilt forward; eyebrows raised, though only in mild surprise. Note especially that stomach muscle control is on MAX. (The added advantage of taking this Pilates approach is that it adds considerable millimetres to one's breast height. Nothing could be better to *ram* the point home.)*

* Note this is one of those occasions where wearing risqué clothing could be a plus.

What makes you think...

...you've got what she wants.

SET THE RECORD STRAIGHT
COMBINATION SEMAPHORE 3

PRACTICE NOTES: We have already suggested that the first semaphore in this combination semaphore should be used frugally. The point of learning to signal correctly is to ensure you get the better of a situation, not become beholden to it.

However, there are times when a little concession is not a bad thing, so learn to minimise the deprecating effect. Note how the model is still smiling. A smile goes a million miles in overcoming adversity. This smile is for *your* benefit, not *theirs*; so, smile from the outside in.

Should you be compelled to use this semaphore we recommend that a visit to the communal bedroom follow immediately. You do not want to stay contrite for too long and it's in the communal bedroom that a recovery manoeuvre always presents itself.*

*And see page 54 for Message Alerts

What I said was...

...only possibly what you thought I said.

SET THE RECORD STRAIGHT
COMBINATION SEMAPHORE 4

PRACTICE NOTES: Having had to execute *Set the Record Straight Combination Semaphore 3*, you've come into the bedroom to execute the recovery manoeuvre (see previous practice notes). He will be lulled into thinking he has a look in. Some chance! This is the "however" to rebuff the earlier reluctant admission, the "but" that neutralises the "and", the "chassé reversé" in an otherwise hopeless dilemma.

In fact, "triumphant" is the word that this combination semaphore immediately brings to mind. Note how righteous our model manages to look as she turns the tables on the situation previously encountered (see page 41).

What I actually said was...

...aren't these *your* newspapers (socks, underwear, coffee cups, condoms) under the bed?

Semaphore #7

APPLICATION: This signal is ideal for repeating the request that you had repeated the day before, and the day before that, and...

SEMAPHORE ACTION: This is a full body signal with arms and hands in thrusting gesture. Position yourself between Recipient and their point of interest (eg: in front of the football on the television or in front of the remote control that activates the football on the television). Back heel should be poised as it is important to appear precarious. You will evoke an immediate response because the Recipient will not savour the prospect of being fallen upon should you topple and thus interrupt the football.

TFS TIP

You'll all recognise the scenario. Since you're not having any luck getting through to them, you get so utterly frustrated you try assertive silence. Wrong move! They're never going to notice you that way. What you need to do is hit them between the eyes with some obvious *Determination* signals.

THE DETERMINATION SIGNALS 1

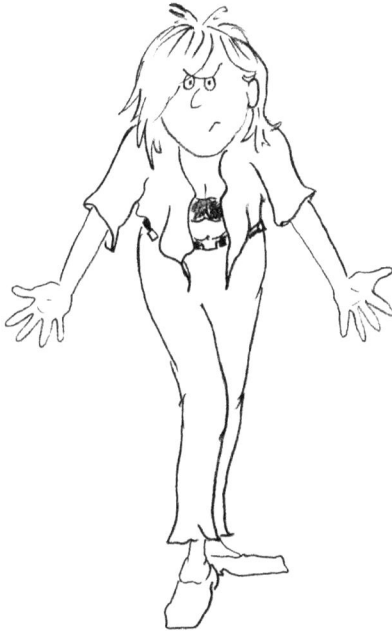

How many times...

INTERPRETATION:
How many times (it's obviously at least 10) do I have to…

Semaphore #8

APPLICATION: Possibly also classifiable as a "desperation signal" this semaphore should pre-empt a reminder that: the clothes haven't left the floor; the leaves are still in the gutter; the knife is still in the jam; the car didn't come home last night; it was my birthday yesterday.

SEMAPHORE ACTION: The elbows are bent. Hands are kept fist-like on hips. Stand straight and facing forward. Thumbs are prominent on waist. **Be well aware Recipients:** Those are PROMINENT thumbs.

Why can't you...?

INTERPRETATION:
How many times (it's obviously at least 20)
do I have to remind you that…

Semaphore #9

APPLICATION: Communicating your needs is critical for preserving your sanity. This semaphore is unquestionably the crucial device for explaining that: you need your privacy; you need your space; you need that home-help you interviewed the other day; it's only your mother you want to have come stay again; some time to yourself might be pleasant.

SEMAPHORE ACTION: Again, bend elbows. However, this time ensure hands are opened and spread with thumbs on back of hip. The expression should be "framed" but not defensive. You are after that "things are OK now but could get a lot worse for you soon" look.

Why can't I...?

INTERPRETATION:
How many times (it's obviously at least 30)
do I have to ask if I might…

Semaphore #10

APPLICATION: This is an ideal signal for warning that you are absolutely adamant that you are not going to be seen any longer as: a walking telephone directory; a whatsisface name supplier; a preprogrammed, automatic event scheduler; or an information technology doormat.

SEMAPHORE ACTION: Collapse forcefully in a double knee bend action and slap left hand on face. (Remember you are only signalling, so be careful not to knock yourself out.) Drop jaw. **Recipients:** Learn CPR before a matter of life and death arises. Your behaviour truly does result in knock-out stuff.

I told you that yesterday!

INTERPRETATION:
How many times (obviously at least one *million*)
am I going to be asked to provide this information?

The TFS Self-absorption Exercise in 4 steps

The determination signals can take it all out of you, can't they? Try these terrific self-absorption exercises. They will help you unwind. They are your affirmations, your support in shaky times.

THE FIRST STEP: Stand in front of the mirror and relax. Breathe deeply. Feel the oxygen reach your extremities. Remember you are a woman and women can do *anything*. Now, start talking to your reflection.

(Below is the *actual* session used by model, Joylene, during which she managed a self-absorption unwind. See how easily she transforms overwhelming anxieties into the normal distractions of womanhood.)

THE SECOND STEP is to do the exercises on the following pages.

MY TRUE SELF-ABSORPTION AFFIRMATION SESSION

I am my own woman!
I am not a walking phone book.
I am not going crazy!
Gosh, I could swear that pimple is less obvious today.
I wonder if my tummy's sticking out as much as it did yesterday?
Damn, I forgot to get that electrolysis done.
What the hell am I doing in front of this mirror?
          signed
                    Joylene
                    Higginbottom

PRACTICE NOTES: The shower, car, or lavatory are wonderful places for self-absorption exercises (if you can get them to yourself). However, it is IMPORTANT not to drive and self-absorb at the same time.

52

1. What did he mean I'm developing meaningful curves?

2. They can't be that bad from behind.

3. Perhaps I could liposuck that bit.

4. And a face lift could look quite good.

Message **Alerts**

Ladies, take note! It is so important to recognise the indicators that call for the use of urgent semaphore. We call these *message alerts* or *explosion points*. These are a warning to you that it's time to limber up and start signalling. Here are some examples of message alerts:

- A hunched teenager makes an appearance in the room.
- The newspapers have reached knee height— but not on your side of the bed.
- You are accused of shouting.
- You thought that you were doing something together but here you are, on your own, still waiting.
- A hunched teenager's clothing makes an aromatic appearance in the room.
- The TV is requisitioned despite the fact that it's Sunday evening.
- The cat's vomit is stepped over in happy oblivion by various fellow-residents.
- A hungry hunched teenager makes an appearance in the room and informs you there is nothing to eat.
- You hear someone ask, "Have you seen…"

Learn to undertake the following semaphores in the face of a message alert. Once a Recipient has learned to recognise the signs at stage 1 they'll do anything you ask to avoid having to witness the hideous signs exercised during stage 3.

① Tolerate

② Cogitate

③ Agitate

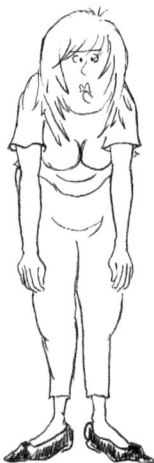

USING FEMALE SEMAPHORE ON SPECIAL OCCASIONS 1 CHRISTMAS

"Guess What! I bring
you tidings of great joy
from the kitchen."

Semaphore #11

APPLICATION: This is the perfect semaphore for those occasions when: life's a bitch but you can't figure out why; life's probably not yet a bitch but it may well be shortly; *life's definitely not a bitch but you're sure as hell determined that you're* going to be one.

SEMAPHORE ACTION: With right shoulder high and arm bent, the left shoulder must slump. Eyes remain focused on middle distance and mouth must stay firmly shut. Keep hands limp and meaningful.

TES TIP

On those occasions when you're not absolutely convinced that your situation merits sympathy but you really think it ought to, it's time to lay it on really thick and signal that you are unquestionably *The Wounded Party*.

I don't expect you'll understand.

INTERPRETATION:
Even though I know you don't know what it is that I think you should know,
I personally think it's time you made sure you got yourself in the know.

Semaphore #12

APPLICATION: Female Semaphorists, use this signal when you're driven to: light the fire and use the TV Guide as kindling; wash the clothes with the teenager's new boyfriend's number still in the pocket; feed the dog the twins' candy for pudding.

SEMAPHORE ACTION: Push lower jaw out, widen eyes and breathe out heavily. Slump shoulders to lowest level of female helplessness. Buckle the knees. Body is a dichotomous mixture of slack and taut. **Recipients:** React rapidly to this semaphore and make sure it's YOU WHO DOES IT—or suffer further gnawing consequences—day, after day, after day, aft...

I guess I'll have to do it.

INTERPRETATION:
I have no confidence that you will do it even though that's what I'm getting at, so I'm just going to martyr myself and make your life a misery later.

Semaphore #13

APPLICATION: A signal of this magnitude should be used to spell out such vital messages as: do join the boss in Bermuda, I'm off to Tiffany's; golf Saturday with the boys is fine, I'll use the time to drive up to the health farm; that's cool—eat the last of the ice cream, I just won't tell where I hid the chocolate.

SEMAPHORE ACTION: Stay focused and sarcastic. Head on one side, eyebrows raised and, with hands warmed by your indignant breast, demonstrate an appearance of cynical acceptance.

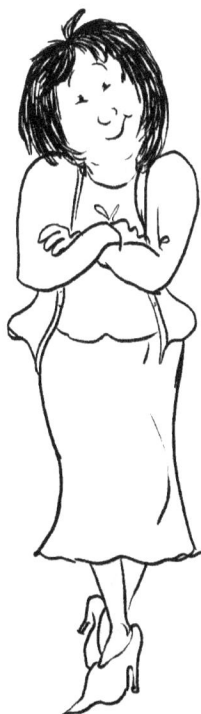

Go ahead!

INTERPRETATION:
You're going to have fun without me and you expect me to be delighted?

You're the Wounded Party
Combination Semaphore 1

PRACTICE NOTES: You are now a fair way to becoming an expert at female semaphore. Note how subtle reverses allow signalling to be extended. Learn to take advantage of your curves to deliver the messages you think the Recipients should be receiving.

Do not be backward when you need to be coming forward.

I don't expect you'll understand but...

...why can't I...

...ever be understood.

You're the Wounded Party
Combination Semaphore 2

PRACTICE NOTES: As much as your experiences would have it otherwise, Recipients are not always stupid. This semaphore shows you how to milk a situation when they are already aware that you may not be feeling your most ecstatic. See how clearly our model follows sarcasm with an air of martyred detachment. If that doesn't lay down a sense of guilt, nothing will.

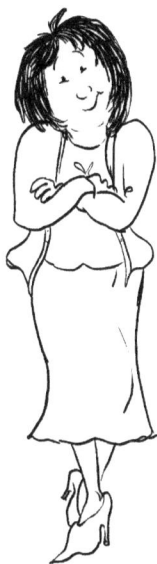

You go ahead...

...I've already organised to be feeling sorry for myself.

Flex the Following Areas of Vulnerability

Nothing's my own any more.

Here I go again shouldering the domestic burden.

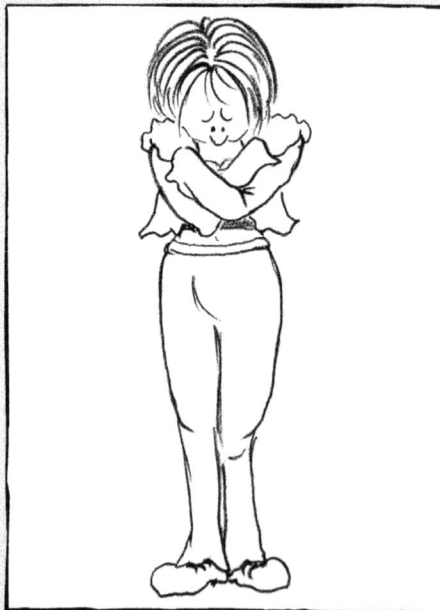

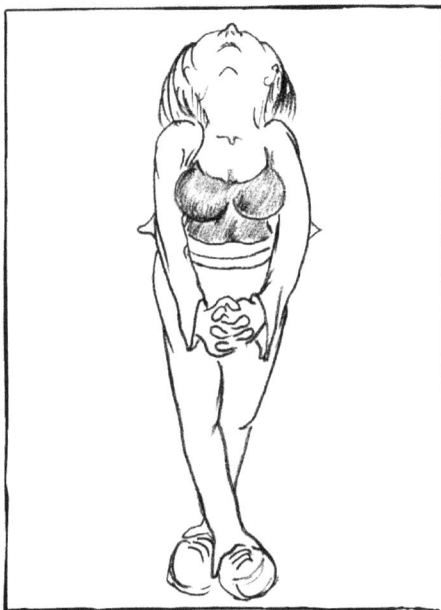

Why am I always being taken for granted.

Oh hell I've just wet my pants.

Self-control

Semaphore #14

APPLICATION: This is the most effective semaphore you will ever learn. Use it liberally to administer such advice as: what a shame, I don't know where you've left the keys; sorry, can't imagine where the remote is; how awful that you've lost your iPhone.

SEMAPHORE ACTION: Body remains open to suggestion, and eyes remain open also, but only just, with considered surprise. Finger raised to lips in ineffective attempt at assisting with the search. Under no circumstances must you join in. (**Recipients:** You're on a hiding to nothing.)

TFS TIP

It's now official—they're so dependent that you'd like to hit the wall...and the roof...and the floor. Well, don't let them get the better of you, girls! There's no need to ricochet. It's time to show them that you are made of sterner stuff and they will never succeed in undermining your *self-control*.

70

I don't know!

INTERPRETATION:
EVEN THOUGH I DO KNOW, I LEARNED LONG AGO NOT TO admit it.

Semaphore #15

APPLICATION: This semaphore should give ample warning that they had better not ask you: the same question for the sixth; seventh; eight; ninth (et seq) time.*

SEMAPHORE ACTION: With feet first anchored in an elevated second ballet position, squeeze yourself into a paroxysm of disbelief. Body remains a bulwark against intrusion while feet are prepared to spiral clockwise to achieve a 360° should further incursions render that necessary.

* Remember ladies, it is not that they haven't heard you, it is simply that you are not giving them the answer they would prefer you to deliver.

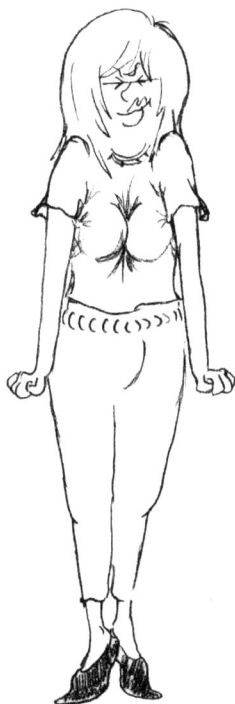

I've already told you!

INTERPRETATION:
Ask me one more time and I'll drill a hole in this floor with my shoes

Semaphore #16

APPLICATION: The irony of this semaphore is that it is always conducted out of sight of the Recipient to indicate resolute defiance in the face of such distant calls as: "Mum!?"; "Darling!?"; "How do you fix the audio on this thing?!"; "Maa-uuuuuummm?!"

SEMAPHORE ACTION: Keep body very erect and taut. Fold arms in determination and fix mouth in "my lips will remain sealed until you come find me" position. **Recipients Note:** (although the whole point of this book is that you never do seem to note) once the Female Semaphorist has this signal learned, you might just as well give up. Those long-distance conversations will get you nowhere.

I said, I can't hear you!

INTERPRETATION:
What do you mean, if you can hear me I must be able to hear you?

Vent the Frustration

Maintaining your self-control leads to inevitable frustration. Giving vent to that frustration is essential. Any competent Female Semaphorist knows how important it is to let off steam.

Here are some activities that are ideal for venting frustration:

Sensible things to do

Phone your best friend to discuss the difficulties.

Dig the new flower garden.

Close your eyes and count to 10.

Pour yourself a cup of tea.

Take the dog for a long walk.

Scream into a pillow.

Far-more-sensible things to do

Phone a friend on the other side of the world.

Buy lots of new clothes for yourself.

Throw the clothes they need for the morning onto the damp towel they left in the corner.

Pour yourself a stiff whisky.

Give the dog the last of the eye fillet.

De-stress Exercises

De-stress exercises are simple and remarkably effective.

First, capture your stress with all available limbs.

Second —LET IT ALL LOOSE!

Using Female Semaphore on Special Occasions 2
Summer Vacation

"Do you think
I need to go on
a diet?"

The Anatomy of The Female Semaphorist

Here's what makes The Female Semaphorist that special person she is.

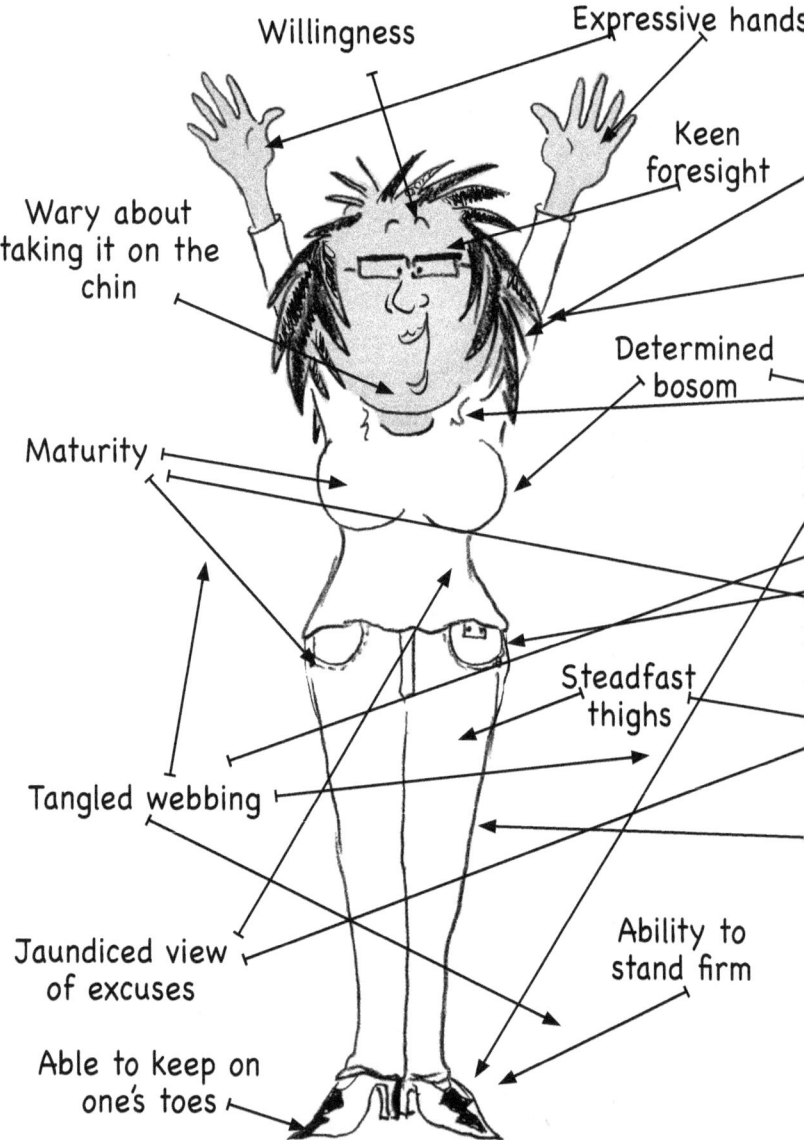

Willingness

Expressive hands

Keen foresight

Wary about taking it on the chin

Determined bosom

Maturity

Steadfast thighs

Tangled webbing

Jaundiced view of excuses

Ability to stand firm

Able to keep on one's toes

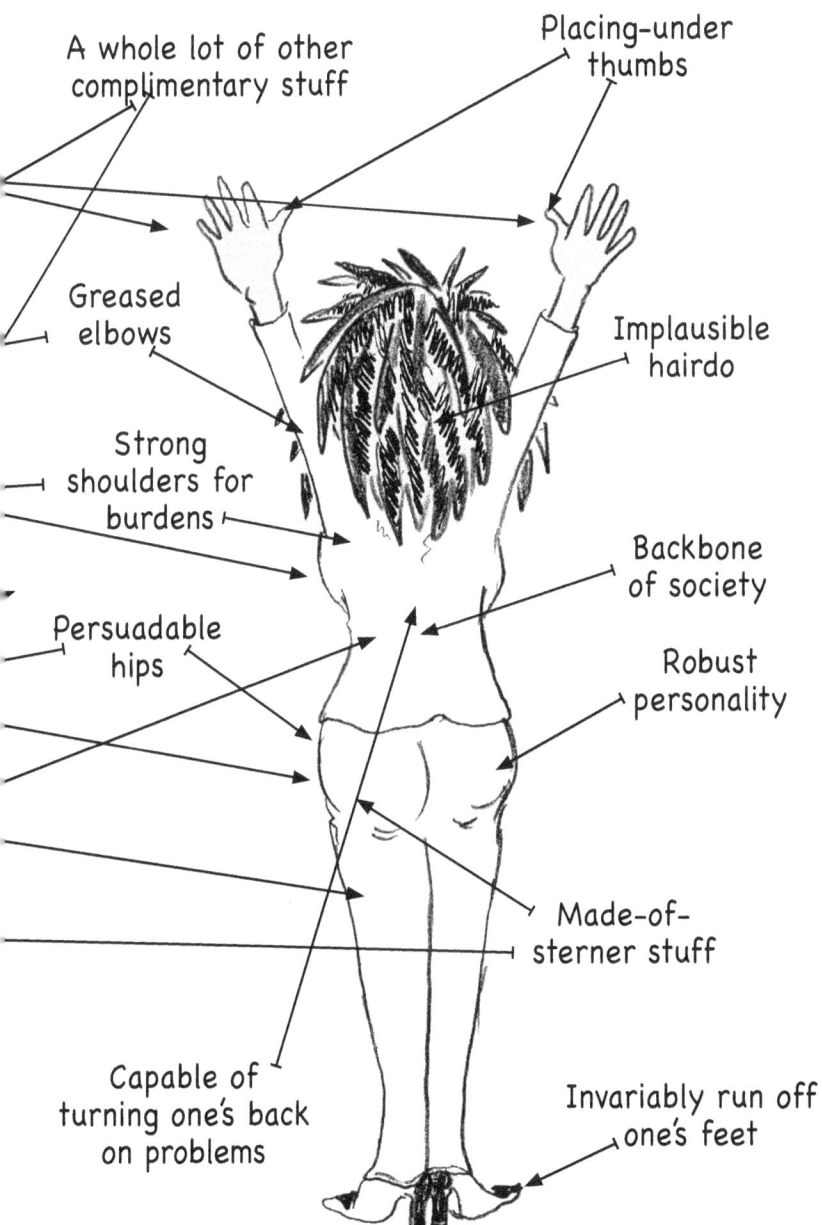

A whole lot of other complimentary stuff

Placing-under thumbs

Greased elbows

Implausible hairdo

Strong shoulders for burdens

Backbone of society

Persuadable hips

Robust personality

Made-of-sterner stuff

Capable of turning one's back on problems

Invariably run off one's feet

Semaphore #17

APPLICATION: Brace yourself with this signal to communicate the fact that they have your permission to bore you rigid concerning: the failure of the ex-boyfriend to call despite her breaking up the relationship; the failure of his boss to increase his pay despite never discussing the issue; the abject failure of Miss Fleming to recognise the obvious merit in the indelible drawing the twins did on the Day Care lavatory wall.

SEMAPHORE ACTION: Arms are folded as in a prelude to something. Arch back slightly and clench buttocks. Exhibit supreme understanding. You will need all the stability and resilience you can muster.

TES TIP

Having gone through so much trauma don't be confused if the benevolent in you makes a sudden appearance. It may be rare but it *is* permitted. Adjust your grimace to a smile, loosen your shoulders, de-weather your brow. It's time to semaphore *Empathy*.

How to Signal Empathy 1

Tell me *all* about it...

INTERPRETATION:
Oh dear…here we go again.

Semaphore #18

APPLICATION: Use this signal so as not to seem disloyal on the occasion your girlfriend*: shows you the new outfit she's bought that's two sizes too small; seeks your reassurance that it was a good idea to book him a surprise holiday in Uzbekistan; tells you the cosmetic surgeon she's booked might not have much experience, but she's getting a great discount.

SEMAPHORE ACTION: Face is wide and smiling in attempt to demonstrate pleasure. Head is tilted as this will disguise any shock. Thumbs and forefingers are massaged to prevent an oral communication you might later regret.

* CAUTION: Be sure not to offend by using this signal with girlfriends who are themselves competent Female Semaphorists.

No, truly. It's great!

INTERPRETATION:
Stupid cow! What did you go and do that for?

Semaphore #19

APPLICATION: Be prepared to sacrifice your equilibrium to signal your absolute loyalty concerning: the continued failure of the ex-boyfriend to phone despite her abusive call to him the night before; the failure of his team to institute a rise to the first division despite discussing the issue very loudly; the abject failure of Miss Fleming to praise the twins' display of creative play during the water fight; the fact that he's terminally ill with the common cold.

SEMAPHORE ACTION: You'll be too exhausted to protect yourself with folded arms—or do anything much, for that matter. Just slump.

HOW TO SIGNAL EMPATHY 3

How awful; do tell me again.

INTERPRETATION:
Do I have to go though this all over again.
(Sometimes translated as: no, go ahead, ruin my day)

The Retrogression of the Female Form

Tell me all about it.

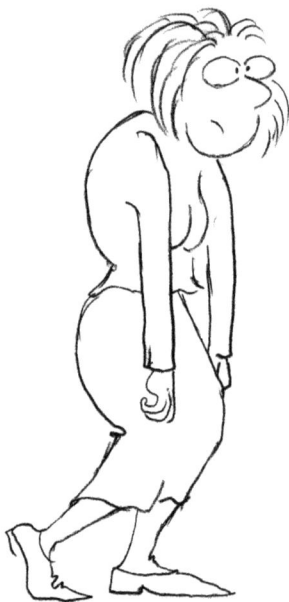

How awful; do tell me again.

Not at all. Not at all. Do tell me again.

Be careful with empathy. Exercising empathy too liberally is a trap for the young female player. Too much empathising can be debilitating and, left unchecked, can lead to the acute retrogression of your female form. Learn to recognise this combination semaphore in your female friends. There is no calcium quick-fix, here, so be ready to run them through the de-stress exercises on page 77 if necessary.

Now it's time to examine the past. Royal women feature frequently in the list of notable Female Semaphorists in history, and the modern woman does well to heed the lessons they teach. Not all have signalled their intentions successfully, but this does not diminish the cautionary value of their particular stories.

Among the most obvious examples in the *unfortunate* category are: Mary Queen of Scots; Anne Boleyn, the second wife of Henry VIII of England; and Marie Antoinette, the only wife of Louis XVI of France. These women may not have been dizzy, but by failing to send the correct signals they certainly lost their heads.

MARY QUEEN OF SCOTS

Mary's problem was not that she was a poor signaller, but that she was sending her signals to a woman—Queen Elizabeth I. Not only that, but she never did manage to get an audience with Elizabeth who, as a consequence, never got to see the signals Mary was sending in the first place. Failing even to get across a decent attempt at *signalling the need to chat*, Mary's frustration boiled over and she resorted to more and more desperate and thus conflicting signals. Mary would have done a whole lot better if she had used *signals that set the record straight*. (See page 20.)

Furthermore, if Mary really did get herself trussed up in the amount of gear shown in the famous portrait of her (*opposite*) it's no wonder she never got the right message across. It would be hard to detect anything much coming out of that lot.

SIGNAL FEMINAE

SIGNAE FEMINAE

ANNE BOLEYN

Anne Boleyn's problems were quite different from Mary's. She was, after all, signalling to her man, Henry VIII, with ample opportunity for an audience—at least in the early days. But in common with Mary, she lost control of her limbs and consequently lost her head. As Shakespeare perceptively observed, it is dangerous to flay one's arms in the presence of a man who feels he's on the back foot—particularly when that man is a royal over-weight:

"Press not a falling man too far!" (Henry VIII Act III, Scene II).

There is plausible evidence, too, that Anne had a sixth finger on her left hand. It was never going to be easy for Henry to get a clear reading from a woman who couldn't even manage a respectable *high five*. On these two counts alone she was signalling a lost cause.

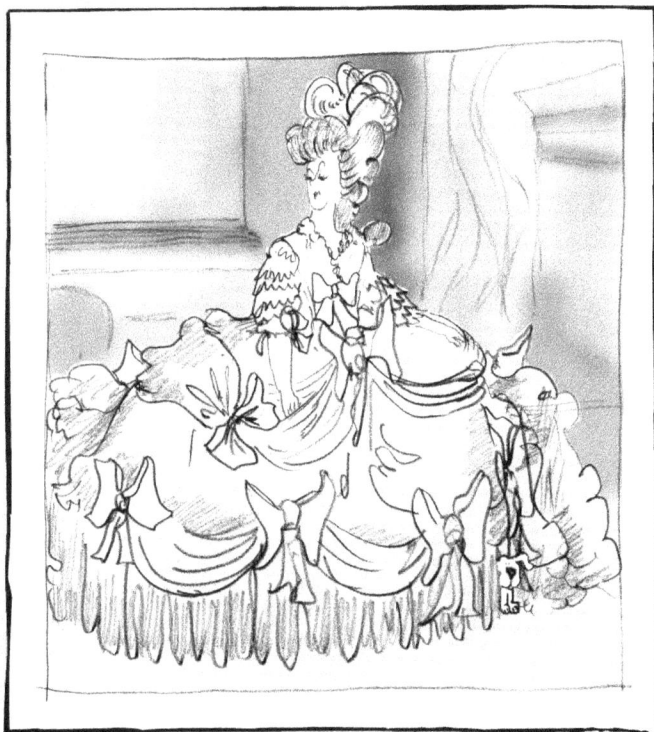

MARIE ANTOINETTE

There is little doubt that Marie Antoinette was doomed from childhood. One of 16 siblings there was always someone standing between her and any hope of clear Female Semaphoric communication. Marrying the portly Louis XVI didn't help. He had enough difficulty seeing his own feet let alone seeing her signals. The ultimate irony for Marie Antoinette, we now know, is that the contemptuous remark *"Let them eat cake"* that is always attributed to the poor woman was never uttered by her at all.

Always misunderstood, Marie Antoinette let her female semaphore skills lapse. Like Mary Queen of Scots she took to hiding behind her own skirts. Unfortunately, she never did learn the difference between the signals "I'm dressed to please" and "I'm dressed to kill".

A more positive lesson in Royal Performance is gained from the example set by Queen Victoria. Not only did Victoria continue to command the affection and *attention* of her husband until his untimely death, but she reigned longer than any other monarch. Quite obviously, she knew exactly what signals to put out and when.

METHOD OF SEMAPHORING BY HAND FLAGS

QUEEN VICTORIA

Queen Victoria honed much of her skill on board the Royal Yacht. Being someone who was not amused, it was important to keep unnecessary noise around her to a minimum. Consequently many orders were given by hand signal. Victoria would observe the crew on these occasions and watch them go about their practice of military semaphore. Although she never said very much to them, being a reasonably loyal royal, she was nonetheless not madly impressed by the ineptitude of some of these men. As can be seen from the example taken from a contemporary chart (above), men are not naturally adapted to semaphore and never seem to know quite where to put themselves. It was a system of communication, Victoria felt, that should be kept as the preserve of women.

Not really a bird to endear herself to others, Victoria cultivated *The Imperial Brush Off.* This signal has less currency these days. However it is useful for the odd occasion—such as when hope is expressed to you that the new boyfriend might be allowed to stay the night.

What better way to garner awe and respect than with the signal *We Are Not Amused.* This signal also has less currency these days. However it is useful for the odd occasion—such as when the fact is presented to you that the new boyfriend did in fact stay the night.

Semaphore #20

APPLICATION: Develop this semaphore in order to indicate that despite reassuring them to the contrary: you really would rather like to be married; sure, living in sin has been fun but an exorbitant white wedding would rather take your fancy; you'd much prefer to pay for that pricey skiing holiday than take the free fishing trip; you think the twins should ideally be a good 12 years older before they start to learn to drive.

SEMAPHORE ACTION: Place hands in complete contradiction to each other. Thus right hand holds neck in defensive posture while left hand gestures extreme laissez faire. The Recipient should not be given the benefit of eye contact.

TFS TIP

You know it, Queen Victoria knew it, and the Recipient knows it, the Serious Female Stuff is always going to be delivered in a series of disguises. That's your female prerogative. Using these signals will ensure they understand what it is that you really think even though you're making every apparent attempt to have them think you believe the opposite. They'll be so confused you're sure to get your own way.

I suppose so.

INTERPRETATION:
I don't suppose so for a minute.

Semaphore #21

APPLICATION: Fertile Semaphorists, this signal will advise those close to you that: your period is only one week away but your tears are invariably much closer; you are on the verge of being unspeakably ghastly—and wallowing in it; how could they even suggest the possibility of PMT; given how much you've had to semaphore lately, it's no wonder you're miserable.

SEMAPHORE ACTION: Your whole attitude must speak of the misused martyr. Hence the chin turns up, the shoulders turn down and the neck elongates with pathos. Eyes are stoic but eyebrows should barely conceal the hurt and/or anger. Arms are folded behind back as a symbol of what is endured through womanhood.

Whatever you say.

INTERPRETATION:
I really can't go along with what you're saying.

Semaphore #22

APPLICATION: This is the perfect warning semaphore when you wish to be assured that: your new stretch jeans were the perfect purchase; the mini skirt makes you look so much slimmer; of course you needed that new piece of jewellery; looks as if combining a new cut, perm and colour was a great cost-saving device.

SEMAPHORE ACTION: Anxiety needs to be left at the door. Head is held high, arms exude embrace and confidence. A poised 'balletic' hand will help polish the deceit. (**Repeat after me, Recipients:** "The jeans are the perfect purchase; the mini skirt does make you look so much slimmer; of course you need that new piece of jewellery; and—indeedy—it does look as if combining a new cut, perm and colour was a great cost-saving device.")

What do you think?

INTERPRETATION:
Whatever you think, only tell me what it is that I *want* you to think.

Signal the Serious Stuff
Combination Semaphore 1

PRACTICE NOTES: Going along with what the Recipient has to say may seem like the best option at the time. The Female Semaphore, however, teaches that honesty is ultimately the best policy. Here is a combination semaphore for you to practice that will give them the true picture despite any earlier apparent complicity in their lunatic scheme.

Whatever you say...

...but how could you have
actually *said* that?!

SIGNAL THE SERIOUS STUFF
COMBINATION SEMAPHORE 2

PRACTICE NOTES: What can we say? Other than that the practice of the second part of this combination semaphore is probably not madly good practice at all—especially given the state of the average 'mature' bosom.

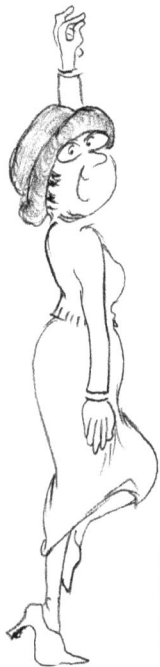

What do you think...

...I've started to Age Defy.

Semaphore #23

APPLICATION: This semaphore is an invaluable way to warn the Recipient that: after three nights in a row you think you've earned a night to read the next chapter...and probably the next; he may not have had a chance to get near you for weeks but can't he see that the book is *still* about to get to an exciting bit.

SEMAPHORE ACTION: This semaphore is all in the facials. Raise one eyebrow and peer sceptically with one eye. Turn smile to tolerant grimace. In every other respect you must remain still and impassive.

TFS TIP

It's time to claim some *me* time, girls, so learn how to signal the *No-Go Zones.* Your soft *inner* self will find it hard not to be your normal *sacrificial* self, but these semaphores deliver the most efficient signals to ensure your equilibrium survives the daily onslaught.

Can't you see...

INTERPRETATION:
Are you blind or something?

Semaphore #24

APPLICATION: Maternal Semaphorists, use this signal as a blunt reminder to your offspring that: you'd actually prefer not to be used as a Bouncy Castle while you're reading the newspaper; you'll just need five minutes concentration to fix the washing machine that's flooding the laundry; it would be really quite a pleasant experience to go to the lavatory without interruption.

SEMAPHORE ACTION: Be aware that there is no gentle way of advising your children that you are your own woman underneath that stoic exterior. Knit your brow into a natural state of desperation, arrange your 'skirt' into a protective barrier, and fix gaze into an unassailable message of self defence.

Can't I even...

INTERPRETATION:
I'm out for the count so push off and leave me ALONE!

No-Go Zone
Combination Semaphore 1

PRACTICE NOTES: We know you have been doing so well. We left off teaching you these *No-Go Zone* semaphores till the last as they will help you to reap the rewards you so amply deserve. Do not let them daunt you. You must not begin to feel that they will sap the superwoman in you. They are, in fact, the key to self-survival.

Note in this combination semaphore how our model retains a degree of friendly tolerance while still managing to issue the rebuff. After all, you don't want to close down all avenues *permanently*.

Can't you see...

...I'll be reading my book tonight.

No-Go Zone
Combination Semaphore 2

PRACTICE NOTES: It is not unknown for some Female Semaphorists to resort to using this full sentence to signal to their pets.

It proves the most effective message, however, when directed at their preschool children.

Why...

...can't I even...

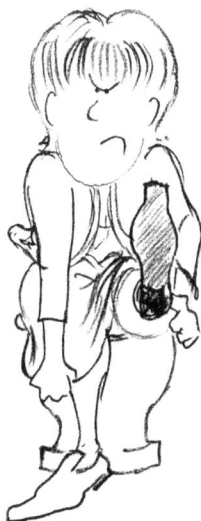
...go to the
lavatory on my own

There will be occasions when Semaphore #23 is insufficient to signal your need for time out. At these times you will need to resort to extreme Female Semaphoric measures. Here we provide a step by step guide that will guarantee you a good night's sleep.

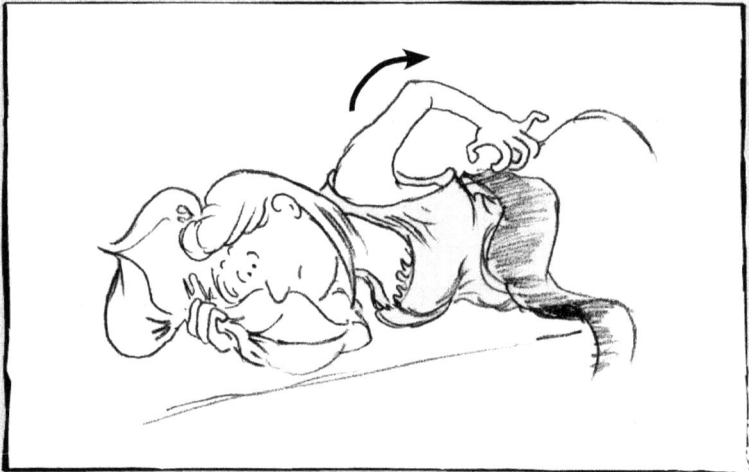

①   Slip silently into bed without
effecting eye contact.
Ascertain position of bedding.

② Moving elbow with assured determination, take good handful and lift toward cold shoulder.

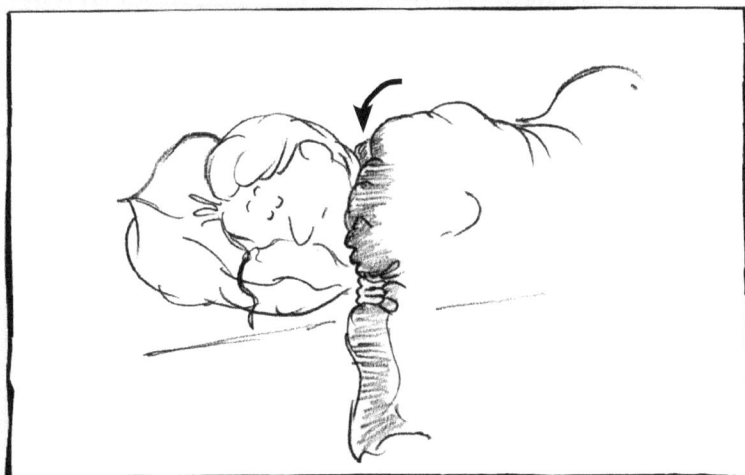

③ Maintain full-wrap position. Bedding is held tightly closed, as are eyes. DO NOT MOVE!

MIXED SEMAPHORES
FOR THE QUALIFIED SEMAPHORIST 1

PRACTICE NOTES: The delivery of mixed messages is part of a woman's more finely tuned arsenal. Sending effective Mixed Semaphores takes considerable skill and is an art which is developed only after years of dedicated practice. The results of such dedication, however, are hugely rewarding. Mixed messages keep Recipients on their toes. They ensure Recipients don't become too relaxed or complacent. Try your hand at jumbling up previously learned semaphores and watch Recipients collapse in a heap of confusion.

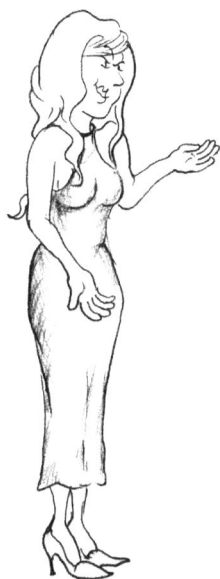

What I actually said was...

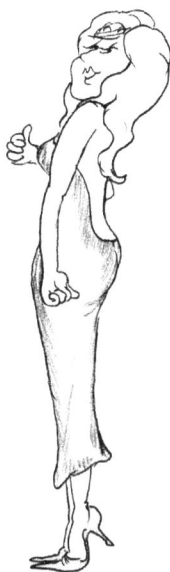

...what makes you think...

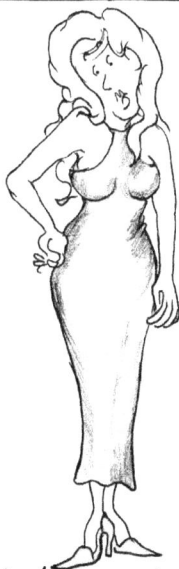

...I don't expect you'll understand!

Mixed Semaphores
for the Qualified Semaphorist 2

PRACTICE NOTES: Here is another of those unexpected little Mixed Semaphore thoughts. See how our model lulls the Recipient into a false sense of security before leaving them totally confused about what it was she was saying. The Recipient imagines this is the unintended effect of feminine fuzziness and will go on to "humour" the model in order to regain some peace and quiet. In fact she has just executed another fine example of shrewd feminine control, and is confident she will now get what she wanted in the first place.

Guess what?

You'll hardly credit...

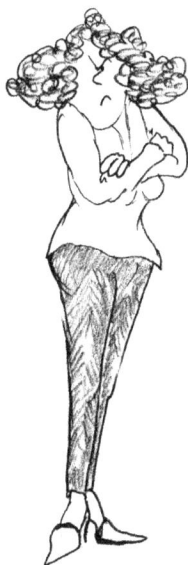

...how moody I can get.

Complex Semaphore for the Qualified Semaphorist 1

PRACTICE NOTES: Another advanced skill is the ability to create a sense of deja vu. Able Female Semaphorists can achieve these subtle communications with the least effort, and yet they find them exceptionally effective in getting their message across. Try it out for yourself watching out all the while for Occupational Over-communication Syndrome.*

* In particularly trying times when Recipients are exhibiting chronic inherent deafness, Occupational Over-communication Syndrome (or OOS as it is known) can become a real hazard for the Female Semaphorist. At these times a TFS Work Out (see page 27) will do wonders to restore one's tired limbs.

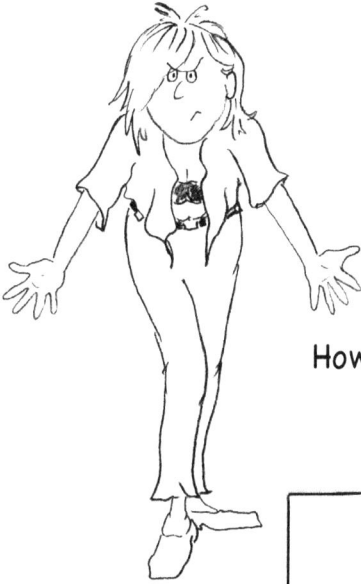

How many times...

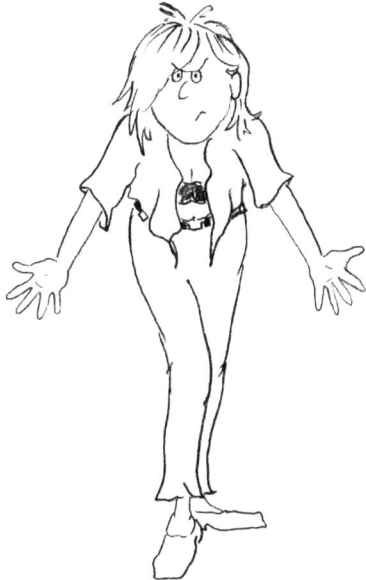

...do I have to
repeat myself?

COMPLEX SEMAPHORE
FOR THE QUALIFIED SEMAPHORIST 2

PRACTICE NOTES: Congratulations. You have all but finished honing your female semaphore skills. Here is a last subtle deja vu device that is guaranteed to drive Recipients to action. This signal combination is known as *The Semaphore Nag*.

Is it just my imagination...

...or have I seen this all before?

Semaphore #25

APPLICATION: Use this signal as your semaphore of last resort to ensure that they really have absorbed what you have wanted to communicate.

SEMAPHORE ACTION: By the time you are driven to use this semaphore you will need all the equilibrium you can muster. Prop hands on knees to maximise support. Brow is deep, eyes are wide, and mouth is steeled. Good luck, ladies, you're probably in for the long haul.

TFS TIP

This is your final lesson, girls. Keep this guide handy for future reference but try to make female semaphore part of your every day. We know it is not always going to be easy to be "heard", so we've included a tears sheet on the final page! If all else fails, draw up your own semaphore battle plan, stick it on the fridge, and burst into tears. They just can't stand *that*.

THE SEMAPHORE OF LAST RESORT

Have you been listening to me?

INTERPRETATION:
Despite all my shouting, gesturing, smiling, weeping, pleading, persuading, gnashing, and downright insisting, why is it that I know you simply have NOT been listening to me?

SHED TEARS ALONG THE DOTTED LINE

Other titles by Margaret Woodhouse:

Humour Non-fiction
Know Your Cat's Purr Points
The 9-Life Habits of Highly Successful Cats
Cats' Tales from Shakespeare
The Latex Cat
The Female Semaphore
Feline Cuisine

Fiction
The Uncertain Measure of Success

Children's Fiction
Jed Bleat for President
Jim Bleat for Prime Minister (!)
The Rise and Fall of Weaseldomderry
And due for release July 2018
Tom the Travel Cat
Little Mister Mischief series

www.ingramcontent.com/pod-product-compliance
Lightning Source LLC
Chambersburg PA
CBHW070812050426
42452CB00011B/2001